ANNUAL EVENTS AND MOMENTS CAPTURED

By

Burt L. Lemen

12808 West Airport Blvd Suite 270M Sugar Land, TX
77478, Unites States

https://www.theempirepublishers.com/

Foreword

Haiku has a Japanese origin with three sentences of 5-7-5 syllables in line order. This book represents a second offering of the types of haiku poetry I have written over the years, and I was encouraged to write a second book. My first book, Sharing Moments of Life and Love, crafted over a lifetime and shared via Haiku Poetry, was well-received and released in early 2025. (On an author's personal note: My Haiku "itch" got started in elementary school when Miss Lane introduced her 5th grade class to this form of poetry. I have been hooked ever since. I have also been asked over the years to write Haiku poems for friends and family for wedding services and for funerals. It seems some of my work has hit some folks in the heart. My hope is that some of these poems can do that for you.)

Dedication

To my Mom and Dad, Mildred and William Lemen Sr., along with my sons, Michael, Matthew, and Mark, and my brother and sister, William Lemen Jr. and Sue Lemen-Paul. Plus, I want to acknowledge a very special, loving, and sweet supportive lady in my life, Denise Moore. You all have all given me inspiration from time to time for the various Haiku topics I have written about over the years.

Dedication Haiku:

Thank you to you all,
What a nice journey I'm on,
Wishing you the best.

Burt L Lemen

Table of Contents

1.0) January Events/Moments

1.1

A new year has dawned,
Wishing you and yours the best,
Make each day special.

1.2

MLK's Birthday,
It is remembered this month,
A Civil Rights Champ.

1.3

January snows,
Seems colder and windier,
Warmer days will come.

1.4

Playing in the snow,
Some kid time shared with adults,
Making snow people.

1.5

The Chinese New Year,
Starts towards the end of this month,
Dragons and parades.

1.6

Winter's still with us,
Warmer days will be coming,
Jack Frost's still nipping.

1.7

New Year's Day parades,
Enjoyed by family and friends,
Nice start to the year.

2.0) February Events/Moments

2.1

February First,
Is National Freedom Day,
A nice stage was set.

2.2

Groundhog Day's a gauge,
For weeks of more snow or not,
A (shadow/sunny) wish made.

2.3

Happy Valentines,
A day shared with our loved ones,
Treat each day with love.

2.4

On Valentine's Day,
Spoil that Sweetie in your life,
A special day shared.

2.5

Canada enjoys,
What's called National Flag Day,
Our Flag Day's in June

2.6

On President's Day,
Remember our Fore Fathers.
Our Country's Stage set.

2.7

It's Mardi Gras time,
Dress up and enjoy some fun,
Parades and marches.

2.8

This month, Ash Wednesday,
A holy day remembered,
Easter is coming.

3.0) March Events/Moments

3.1

Daylight saving time,
Enjoy that extra hour,
With family and friends.

3.2

Make sure to wear green,
Avoid getting those pinches,
On Saint Patrick's Day.

3.3

The first day of Spring,
A very nice reminder,
Warm days are coming.

3.4

March Madness is here,
Basketball heaven for some,
Parties for others.

3.5

Preseason baseball.
MLB new season starts,
Post-season dreams start.

3.6

For some snow's ending.
Starting to get warmer temps,
Getting a Spring tease.

4.0) April Events/Moments

4.1

April showers bring,
May flowers with more yard work.
What's wrong with winter?

4.2

Major League Baseball,
The games played now count for real,
How will our team(s) fare?

4.3

Scoreboard watching starts.
With our favorite baseball team(s),
Time with family shared.

4.4

It's April Fool's Day.
It's a prankster's holiday,
Enjoy, have some fun.

4.5

Hey, pull my finger,
Time for an April Fool's joke,
I stuck out my tongue. (-Or- Time to fart around)

4.6

There are many days,
Tied to Easter Holiday,
Remember Jesus.

4.7

Earth Day's in this month,
Give a hoot and don't pollute.
Said a wise old owl.

4.8

Celebrate Earth Day,
Do something different today,
Recycle something.

5.0) May Events/Moments

5.1

Don't forget your Mom,
Mother's Day occurs mid-month,
Time is a great gift.

5.2

A day does not pass,
Where I pause to think of Mom,
Happy Mother's Day,

5,3

My Mothers now gone,
But she remains in my heart,
Mom, you are still loved.

5,4

Family memories shared,
Especially on Mom's Day,
Take time to reflect.

5.5

Armed Forces Day gets
celebrated in this month,
Our troops keep us safe. (-Or- Remember our
troops.)

5.6

Take time to honor,
Our Service Men and Women,
Memorial Day.

5.7

Memorial Day,
A day to honor our troops,
They ensure freedom.

5.6

Some gave it their all,
Because freedom is not free,
Remember our troops.

6.0) June Events/Moments

6.1

Flag Day is mid-month,
Take time to honor our flag.
Start of our Nation.

6.2

Fathers help to guide,
Setting firm but loving bounds,
Father's Day draws near.

6.3

Spend time with your Dad,
More than just on Father's Day,
Make some nice memories.

6.4

Share Father's Day time,
With your Mom and siblings too,
Time is a great gift.

6.5

First day of Summer,
Happens later in this month,
Enjoy the outside.

6.6

The start of Summer,
Enjoy this season's beauty,
Nature's wake-up call.

6.7

It's barbeque time.
Fire up the grill, gather 'round,
Smoke-kissed meats and greens.

6.8

Time to get outside,
Try to enjoy nature's best,
Behold the beauty.

6.9

Juneteenth celebrates,
Slavery's end in this country,
Freedom for us all.

7.0) July Events/Moments

7.1

On 4th of July,
Remember this day's founding,
This country's special.

7.2

It is fireworks time,
The night sky bursts into flame,
History remembered.

7.3

The first of July,
Up North, it's Canada Day,
A neighbor's well wish.

7.4

Wow, it's hot outside,
Time for sprinklers and the pool,
Take time to cool off.

7.5

Summer school for some,
Take advantage of this time,
Learn something brand new.

7.6

Stargazing is fun,
Learn about constellations,
Family fun enjoyed.

7.7

It's shorts and tee time,
Work to stay cool in summer,
Dog days of summer.

8.0) August Events/Moments

8.1

Summer still hangs on,
August is still a hot month,
Fall is coming soon.

8.2

Schools getting ready,
To start back up for the Fall,
New school year learning.

8.3

Late summer time shared,
Taking that late vacation,
Fun and memories made.

8.4

Barbeque enjoyed.
Bring out those special dishes,
Friends and Family time.

8.5

Mid-month's a new moon,
Summer nights are filled with stars,
Take time to stargaze.

8.6

Dog days of Summer,
Finally coming to an end,
Fall's around corner.

9.0) September Events/Moments

9.1

Labor Day occurs,
At the beginning of month,
Enjoy this work break.

9.2

Fall days are starting,
Jacket weather is starting,
Enjoy Fall fires.

9.3

Schools are back online,
Enjoy this year of learning,
Work with your teachers.

9.4

School bells are ringing,
Kids are going back to school,
Ah, a parent's break.

9.5

During this Fall month,
National Grandparents Day,
Happens on the 10th.

9.6

The first day of Fall,
Happens at this month's ending,
Enjoy these cool days.

9.7

Tree leaves are changing.
They are losing their color,
And fall on the ground.

10.0) October Events/Moments

10.1

On Columbus Day,
Pause to remember our start,
New World discovered.

10.2

The Canadians,
Enjoy a Thanksgiving too,
On October 9th.

10.3

Happy Halloween,
Pumpkins and trick-or-treaters,
Enjoy this fun time.

10.4

Charlie Brown special,
A nice Halloween moment,
Avoid the rock treats.

10.5

Scary movie time,
Chills and thrills shared with family,
Enjoy the classics.

10.6

Carve that scary face.
On the side of that pumpkin,
Happy Halloween.

10.7

It's getting colder,
There is a cold nip in the air,
Jacket weather now.

11.0) November Events/Moments

11.1

It's early snow time,
Winter weather creeping in,
Time for coats and boots.

11.2

On Thanksgiving Day,
Give thanks for life's positives.
They're all around us.

11.3

Pilgrims remembered,
What a perilous journey,
A New World founded.

11.4

Take time to give thanks,
We live in a special place,
It's land of the free.

11.5

Special meals enjoyed,
With special friends and family,
Holiday cooking.

11.6

Winter Holidays,
Really start with Thanksgiving,
Enjoy these moments.

11.7

Daylight saving time,
Will come to an end this month,
Nighttime comes sooner.

12.0) December Events/Moments

12.1

It is amazing,
The stories told of loved ones,
At holiday meals.

12.2

Santa comes this month,
Were you a good boy or girl?
For this whole past year?

12.3

Time to write Santa,
That special year-end letter,
A Christmas wish list.

12.4

I have a wish list,
Health for our friends and family,
Enjoy this season.

12.5

Happy Holidays,
Take time for those we hold dear,
Time is a great gift.

12.6

We all know Scrooges,
Don't become one this season,
Become Bob Crachet.

12.7

It's Jesus' birthday,
Merry Christmas to you all.
Take time to give thanks.

12.8

Twelve days of Christmas,
A nice song for the season,
A song of true love.

12.9

Pause to remember,
What makes this season special,
It's more than just gifts.

12.10

Wishing a Merry,
Christmas to you and family,
Happy Holidays.

13.0) Throughout the Year Events/Moments

13.1 Happy Birthday

13.1.1

Oh, how time sure flies,
We're another year older,
Hope for wishes, too.

13.1.2

Wishing you the best,
Enjoy that cake and ice cream,
On your special day,

13.1.3

Sing Happy Birthday,
To those special "boys" and "girls",
No matter how old.

13.2 Someone's Getting Married

13.2.1

I am very happy,
Someone wants to marry me,
Two becoming one.

13.2.2

It takes time to find,
That very special someone,
That you want to marry.

13.2.3

A new family starts,
As the "I Do's" are spoken,
Help this couple grow.

13.2.4

A marriage contract,
Can easily be broken;
Work to keep it sound.

13.3 The Birth of a Child

13.3.1

A bundle of joy,
A newborn baby has come,
Enhancing our lives.

13.3.2

Generation next,
Family traditions live on,
Young ones learn quite fast.

13.3.3

I saw a first step,
Young ones really grow up fast,
I heard some words too.

13.3.4

I gaze upon you,
I wonder what you're thinking,
You gave me a smile.

13.4 I Got a New Job

13.4.1

My formal school years,
Finally, are paying off,
Never stop learning.

13.4.2

A means to an end,
Are what jobs can provide us,
Save for rainy days.

13.4.3

Enjoy your new job,
Continue to learn new things,
Knowledge is power.

13.4.4

A job's daily grind,
Supports the cost of living,
Please remember that.

13.5 Retirement

13.5.1

Retire from one's job,
Do not retire from life,
Enjoy and live life.

13.5.2

My daily routine,
Has sure changed with more free time,
Do something special.

13.5.3

My schedule is mine,
I can do what I want now,
What a nice feeling.

13.5.4

Make each day special,
Like it is a holiday,
And pay it forward.

13.6 Friend or Loved One Moving to a Nursing Home

13.6.1

Take time to visit,
With those people you hold dear,
Time is the best gift.

13.6.2

We're on life's highway,
All highways have slower lanes,
Slower's not so bad.

13.6.3

Don't stay down too long.
Find the positives in life,
That keeps you engaged.

13.6.4

Work to stay active,
That supports being healthy,
Even in this home.

13.6.5

Support the helpers,
Who spends time with the Seniors,
In these special homes.

13.6.6

Visit the Seniors,
Who make nursing homes their homes,
Make time to visit.

13.7 Death of a Friend or Loved One

13.7.1

You know you are old,
When your friends start to pass on,
Please remember them.

13.7.2

The River of Life,
Can refresh and cleanse the soul,
Take time to get wet.

13.7.3

Mom, Dad, we miss you,
You both are still remembered,
And very much loved.

13.7.4

A Loved One passes,
There's a lot of firsts that year,
It takes time to heal.

13.7.5

We all get older,
It's sad that Father Time wins,
Here's to a long life.

13.7.6

Remember those folks,
Who are no longer with us,
Share special memories.

Back Page –

Annual Events and Moments Captured via Haiku Poetry

I would like to thank you for taking the time to purchase and read the poems in this book. After the release of my first book, several friends and family members asked me if a second book was in the works. It seems I am always writing haiku poems for special occasions. I have had some health issues lately, and this book, along with my first offering, represent "bucket list" items for me. I want to wish you nothing but the best and my hope is that if any of these haiku poems resonate with you or serve as "food for positive thought", please take the time to "pay it forward" with family and friends. Time spent with loved ones is a very special gift.

Parting Haikus

Thanks for your support,
I don't take things for granted.
Each day is a gift.

I hope this book will,
Make a new life-long ripple,
In your pond of life.

Life is fast enough.
Pause to enjoy special times,
Enjoy these memories.

www.ingramcontent.com/pod-product-compliance
Lightning Source LLC
Chambersburg PA
CBHW070957120626
46546CB00004B/1658